The Innkeeper

The Innkeeper

Gerald Robison

Copyright©2025 by Gerald Robison. *The Innkeeper.*

Published by Parrhesia Publishing and Imprint of Leadership Books, Inc. Las Vegas, NV – New York, NY

LeadershipBooks.com

ISBN: 978-1-965401-94-1 (Hardcover)
978-1-965401-95-8 (Paperback)

Dedication

This book is dedicated to Hannah, Jacob, Beth, Seth, Caleb, Emily, Gracie, Niklaus and Josiah. These are my grandchildren and great-grandchildren.

It is my heart's desire that you come to know Jesus and the gracious way He removes our sin to reconnect us with God the Father.

Once that happens, I hope your vision and understanding of Christmas is more joyful than ever!

Foreword

While serving with Walk Thru the Bible for 36 years I've known many rewards and met so many followers of Christ I am privileged to know. I've visited places I never thought I would go! I did, after all, grow up on Smith Drive in Normal, Illinois — hardly known as a launchpad for global exploration.

Last year Walk Thru the Bible shared God's Word in 141 countries. Even though I've visited a fraction of those nations, I've enjoyed a front row seat to witness the message of God's grace and truth crisscrossing all sorts of barriers from languages and cultures to political systems and economic strata, church denominations, and generations.

In many ways, I've followed in the footsteps of my friend, Gerald Robison, who has been part of Walk Thru the Bible even longer and served as one of our earliest pioneers. Gerald took our innovative live events and transformational biblical resources beyond the United States to the ends of the earth.

Gerald taught me the easiest way to connect cross-culturally is to stick closely to the holy text of Scripture and let God speak for Himself. He also taught me how to help others "step into the story" for themselves. You've likely heard people say, "the devil is in the details." While the sentiment behind that statement is often true, Gerald helped me discover the greater truth: "the divine is in the details." Ironically, sticking close to the actual words of the Bible is the best way to release our imaginations to see the sights, hear the sounds, feel the emotions, and sense the significance of what we read.

The Innkeeper is a beautiful example of setting one's imagination free through the discipline of repeated reading and diligent study. The story, as told by Gerald, will captivate children and fascinate adults who have collected a lifetime of Bible knowledge.

As you turn the pages, you truly will "step into the story" as you travel back in time while discovering insights that are more current than tomorrow's newspaper. You'll be guided each step of your journey by an experienced and trustworthy guide who will introduce you to the story of Jesus through the eyes of an often overlooked and frequently misunderstood innkeeper who has so very much to teach each of us.

So, what are you waiting for? Turn the page and start your new adventure!

Phil Tuttle
President & CEO
Walk Thru the Bible

Prologue

It's been a popular phrase for Christians over the last 20 to 30 years to say, "Don't take Christ out of Christmas!" or "Jesus is the reason for the Season." What they mean is, "Don't try to separate the person of Jesus from the celebration of his birth."

Christmas isn't a "season" – it's a holiday. But when I say that, I don't mean it's simply taking time off from work. No, the word "holiday" means it's a "holy day." It's a day of interaction with God.

Throughout Christmas celebrations around the world, there's no escaping the usual nativity scenes with Mary, Joseph, the baby Jesus, the shepherds, wise men, donkey and other assorted animals. But maybe we have found ourselves retelling the story with imaginations that fill in details not mentioned in the original story. And what about the important details the Bible does give us, but we don't include or mention them in our retelling?

Through the eyes of the Innkeeper we will look more closely at the story of scripture and less to our imaginative traditions. This time let's read the Christmas story from another perspective and discover what else may have happened and what else we may have missed.

Table of Contents

Dedication   7

Foreword   9

Prologue   11

Table of Contents   13

The Innkeeper   15

Searching for More   16

A Wary Invitation   18

A Curious Detour   20

A Legacy of Villainy   22

The Story Reimagined   24

The Story Retold   26

The Innkeeper's Story   28

The Priestly Shepherds   30

The Perfect Lamb   35

Swaddling the Lamb   37

Celebration of the Lamb   38

The Tower of the Flock at Migdal Eder   40

Foreshadow of the Lamb   42

Just Like a Perfect Lamb   44

Joseph and the Innkeeper   46

The Innkeeper Makes Room   48

Making Room for the Lamb   50

About the Author   52

Other Works by This Author   54

List of Illustrations   55

About the Illustrator Jordan Blackstone   56

Back Cover Summary   58

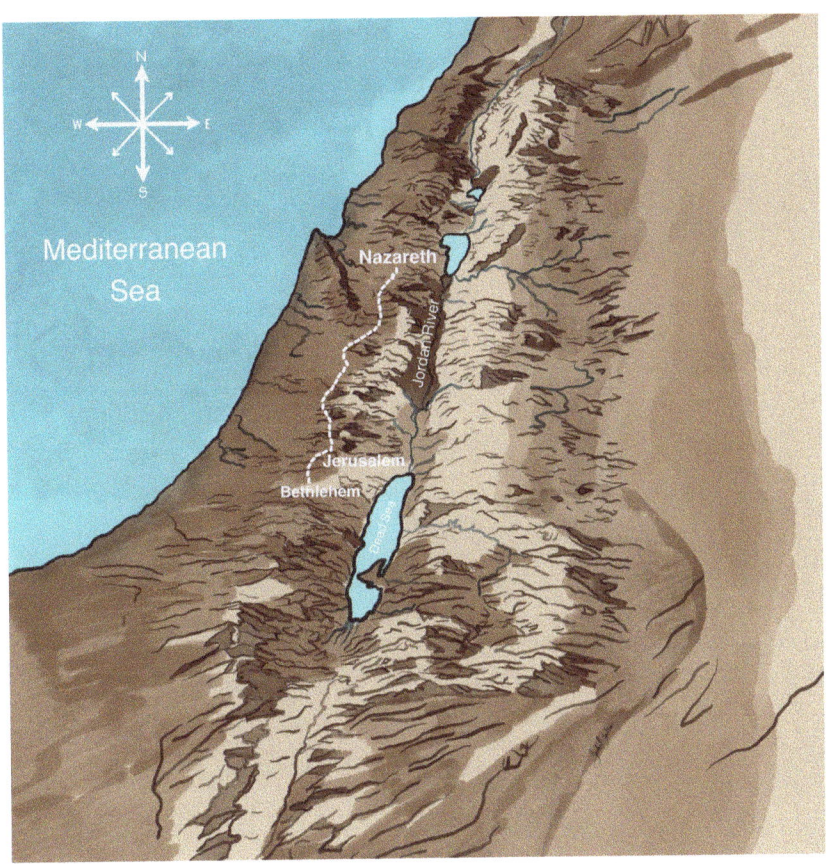

The Innkeeper

"Vilified! Vilified!" retorted the old man with resounding strength in his voice. His eyes reflected a fire of passion erupting straight from his heart. His lips tightened like a vice, tighter and tighter with each turn of his long, long, memory. He was certain—more than certain—that his version of the story was right, and the popular opinion formed over 2,000 years was wrong.

Searching for More

Just four weeks earlier, I sat in my American church, listening to another Christmas sermon – one of the many I'd both heard and given throughout my life. That was before my excursion to the Holy Land.

Thanksgiving had just passed, and the pastor began his sermon by asking, "Who were the two greatest villains in the Christmas story? "Pastor and the audience named the obvious Christmas story villains of Herod (for plotting to kill all young Jewish boys after the birth of Christ), and the Innkeeper, for turning Joseph and Mary away to the stable.

Nothing new here. The same story told the same way, year after year. But this year was different. This year I needed to *feel* something. I needed to *hear* something or *see* something different. I longed for something of actual substance and essence. But so far, it was Christmas as usual. I had nothing.

This year I was determined; I needed Christmas to be something more. So I travelled to the scene. I journeyed to Bethlehem. So what? Tourists go to the Holy Land every day, and this year I would be just one more.

What could be said that had not been said? What could be written that had not been written? What could I find that had not been found? I had only arrived, but so far, I had nothing. I had nothing in my mind, nothing in my heart, nothing that screamed, "This is what you are looking for!"

I was just one more sheep in the flock of camera-laden, sunglass-wearing visitors. Day by day, from hotel to the tour bus, we heard the guides give their standard talks in hopes of generous tips. Some guides were more informative, some more humorous, but while each had insightful bits of history or culture, I found nothing dramatically fresh and sensational. Maybe it would not be? Maybe all that I've heard is all that there is?

Today's bus was more rickety than usual, the dust more voluminous than usual, and the weather more inhospitable than usual. I had a seat by myself and kept the window cracked open to offset the overly warm one-setting heater on the old bus.

We coasted to another stop, where I made my way from the bus to the trinket shops and listened to the chattering of young children selling postcards, "Just one dolla', one American dolla'! Look, look at the pictures! Bethlehem, Jerusalem, Holy Land!" They shouted with desperation to sell their inventory.

Desperation indeed. These dirty munchkins descended like vultures fighting over roadkill. Each one saying anything and showing everything they had to obtain another greenback that would help put fruit or meat on the family table. And, if they couldn't sell you something, they tugged, motioned, and gestured to us toward their favorite shops where they might get a cut on your purchase.

A Wary Invitation

One little boy caught my eye. Smaller and younger than the others by two to three years, he was clearly learning the trade. His timid voice and lack of "showmanship" showed a weakness that drew me to him. I think he read my face, and while he was younger than the others, he'd learned enough to spot my weakness too.

He approached me silently, with cards in his hands. The drone of voices faded as tourists scattered to various sites and shops. Soon we stood there alone. He just looked up at me, waiting for me to say the first words.

I was thirsty, so I asked the lad where I could buy a soda. I was feeling generous – as well as feeling pity for him – so I thought I'd surprise him and purchase one for each of us. While I clasped my camera in one hand, he took my other hand and led me to the streetside shop where he'd obviously earned a coin or two for bringing in a customer.

The shop was made for tourists with dozens of bins lining the outside, mounded with trinkets and toys. A small door made for a cozy entry, while also making it less easy to leave. Wall-to-wall counters inside were filled with olive wood handcrafts, T-shirts emblazoned with "BETHLEHEM" or "Holy Land," and endless postcards, leather bags, belts, shot glasses, bumper stickers, jewelry, and more.

Unfortunately, I could not even get to the door. The bins blocked the semblance of a sidewalk, and the crowd was thicker than usual. On top of that, a tour bus pulled in and unloaded its passengers who eagerly scurried and hurried in, making it impossible to get in, much less find a seat at the counter to order my cola.

Young Jesus at my side (I did not know what else to call him, and the name just slipped into my imagination) saw my disappointment and my need, but there was little he could do for me.

I could not get into this shop... or any others in the seeable distance. So I began to look for a place, any place, that was not crowded and would allow me to rest. I decided the best course of action might be in the opposite direction of the buzzing crowds.

Then Jesus motioned for me to follow him down an alley. A flood of uneasy thoughts crowded my mind. *Was this little Jesus getting ready to rob me? Does he think he's David, and I'm Goliath? Is he leading me to his older brothers who might jump me, take my camera, rough me up, force out my wallet, and leave me as a backstreet tourist statistic?*

I felt this journey starting to take its toll on me. I needed to rest and recuperate. *I could do just as well on my own,* I thought. I thanked my little guide, gave him a generous gift to help appease his father, and sent him on his way.

A Curious Detour

I had sore feet, dry eyes, and a parched throat with no relief in sight. I needed a place to sit, relax, gather my thoughts, and resign myself to disappointment – that this Christmas would be the same as always.

"There!" I spotted a place, behind the storefronts, out of traffic's way. I made one right turn, followed by another, and then a left. In between two shops, I made my way through a thin alley, toward what appeared to be a dead end. My curiosity led me to spot an ever-so-small opening just wide enough to squeeze through. I crouched down and waddled, duck-like, to pop out on the other side.

On the other side was ... well, nothing! *Where did it go? What about the place I spotted from the other side?* All I beheld was a small rock structure hidden at the backside. *Was that it?* It looked bigger and more ... well, it just looked "more" from a distance. This wasn't even worthy of a picture on my digital camera.

Okay, it's not the Taj Mahal, I told myself, *but it's away from the hustle and bustle, and maybe I can just revive myself in a moment of relaxing.*

With soft strides, I approached the little rock building. The closer I got, the more defined became the odor that assailed my senses. I stepped inside the unlit structure and waited a minute for my eyes to adjust from the brightness of the sun on the surrounding whitewashed buildings. As my pupils dilated, I could see that there wasn't much to see here.

As I adjusted to the darkness, a feeble voice spoke. But it did not seem to be directed at me, as it wasn't in a language I understood. Then came the words I could understand.

"Sit. You sit," a voice told me abruptly. This was not the youthful voice of little Jesus – this voice sounded more senior, with a somewhat feeble quality of many years behind him.

He moved closer to me and as spots of light began to light the room, I could make out his visage. He had the weathered appearance and qualities every bit like my imagination of a Bible character. But he was not a character actor, dressed for the tourist's lens, he was simply himself.

His words came slowly and in English with a thick accent. "Not to worry," he continued. "Please sir, you can relax for a few precious minutes. You're welcome to sit and leave once you've been refreshed. There's a bit of water over there."

The old man pointed to the hewn rock bowl on the other side of the room. "I'd be more hospitable and get it for you myself, but the years have taken their toll on me. There was a time I used my ability to serve others, but my body doesn't allow it so much anymore."

A Legacy of Villainy

"Where are we?" I asked.

"This is just where I like to spend my time with a few of my little friends," he said as he pointed to two lambs, and a goat resting in the far corner and his donkey tethered outside the door.

"The town gets so full and busy that there's no room for someone like me, so I just spend my time here. I used to run one of the local hotels, but now my grandson and his wife have taken over the business."

"A hotel?" I said. "That must be one very lucrative business here!"

"It's all a headache," he responded, and he kept talking. "Too many people, too many demands, too many expectations, and not enough money."

"You mean you were an innkeeper? In Bethlehem? You've got to be kidding!" I laughed aloud. "You must have been the butt of a lot of jokes!"

But my eyes were not met with merriment or laughter. The old man just sat there, and his eyes instead met mine with a mixture of both anger and moisture. He looked indignant, as though I had just pierced his heart in an all-too-familiar way – a way he had known a thousand times before.

Suddenly, my own laughter stopped. I had caused this man pain – me and many others like me. His countenance reflected deep grief in his heart, and I knew that he knew something I did not understand.

Was he only tired of being likened to the villain in the Christmas story? Were there just too many jokes with him on the receiving end?

His bottom lip quivered and then quivered again, like the aftershocks of an earthquake. Then he muttered, "Vilified." Softly at first and then louder, he broke out, "Vilified!" I watched as his emotional dam began to break, and a pent-up flow of emotional dross erupted from his soul. Year upon year, decade upon decade, millennia after millennia of ridicule had taken its toll.

"Vilified!" he shouted this time. "Vil-i-fied! Vil-i-fied!" Now his eyes took on a new frame. He seemed stronger now, not the weakened, feeble man I initially met. A fire erupted in his soul like that of a man unjustly accused and sentenced in the court of popular opinion.

"Whoa … whoa … simmer down," I cautioned as I squirmed in my chair. "I'm sorry if I've offended you!"

"Sorry?" he quipped. "As if those five letters wrapped in two syllables can replace the ages of anguish I've suffered … my father, his father, and our fathers before?"

Then he caught himself as though his body had just whispered in his ear to remind him of its age – as though he could not contain the fervor of his indignation. His body quaked and shook, and I reached out a hand to steady him and help him find his seat again.

Tears mounted at the corners of his eyes and then let loose. They ran like streams down the dust of his face to the edge of his beard disappearing into the forest of his full gray beard.

The Story Reimagined

"Have you ever read that story?" he asked. His eyes begged for an answer. "Yes, sure. Hasn't everyone?" I replied.

"Tell me what you know and what you've been told," the old man demanded.

And so, I began retelling the story I'd been told, the one I told others, and the same one I've heard retold to a new generation.

Mary and Joseph made their way to Bethlehem. She was pregnant and near her delivery date, so she rode a donkey while her betrothed husband, Joseph, walked. When they arrived in Bethlehem, they tried to get a room at the inn, but the innkeeper turned them away, saying there was no room for them.

There was always doubt as to whether there really was room or not. Many a preacher waxed on and on about the possibility of there being room, but the miserly innkeeper would not allow them to stay. He turned them away but offered a place in the barn where they could stay with the animals, and Jesus was born there amid the outcast creatures and laid in a manger.

Yes, for as long as I can remember, the second great villain in the Christmas story was the innkeeper! Why didn't he make room for them? Why didn't he send his own teenage children to the barn and make room in his heart and his inn for this overdue woman who obviously needed a place of care for the impending birth of a baby? How could he do that? How cold and heartless he must have been.

"Read it again," said the old man, tears still limping downward, some making it through the forest and falling from the ends of his beard.

"Read it again!" he said more forcefully.

I reached into my pocket and pulled out the little Bible I was accustomed to carrying every day of this trip – just to stay in tune with the guides. But this time I looked at the words more carefully – more studiously.

And there I read aloud from the Gospel according to Luke, chapter 2 and verse 7 ... "And she brought forth her firstborn son, and wrapped him in swaddling clothes, and laid him in a manger; because there was no room for them in the inn."

The old man's English was good enough to follow my reading of the story, but he did not need to. He had heard the story often enough and studied it deeply enough that he had it memorized well.

The Story Retold

"There," he said. "There you have it!"

"There I have what?" I countered.

With a knowing glint in his eye, he insisted, "Tell me of the conversation between Joseph and the innkeeper! Tell me how it says he begged for a room, but the Grinch of the original Christmas wouldn't open a room! Show it to me!"

"Well ... it's not there. The story doesn't go into much detail," I said.

He continued, "Tell me how it was when you stepped off your tour bus and you wanted to enter a shop for refreshment. Tell me about your conversation with the store owner, and how he turned you away."

"I didn't even get in the shop," I said in a way to defend myself. Besides, what did this have to do with the innkeeper?

"Exactly!" the old man snipped. "You didn't even get inside, did you?"

"Well ... no—" I wanted to continue, but he interrupted.

"Tell me now – and thousands of others – of how this man offended you and turned you away!"

"But he didn't," I said.

"Then why have generations told the innkeeper story as if there had been a conversation between him and Joseph? Why do you think the innkeeper even knew there was a pregnant woman on a donkey outside?"

"Let me tell you the story as my father was told by his father, who was told by his father, back through the ages to the original day in question."

And the old man seemed to relax as he told the story passed down through his family, and the story he passed on to his son and grandson as they carried on as innkeepers in Bethlehem.

The Innkeeper's Story

"Yes, Caesar Augustus had decreed a tax, and that required a census. Every family had to return to their roots, and that included Joseph and his espoused wife, Mary. She was pregnant and ready to give birth when they arrived in Bethlehem. The trip had been long and tiring for people of all ages, but for a nine-month pregnant woman, it's a wonder she made it at all.

"Relieved to see the lights of Bethlehem in the distance, they grew elated as they realized their difficult trip of 80 miles was nearly over. But they hadn't counted on the crowds here in this sleepy village. It seems that Bethlehemites had multiplied freely, and now everyone was back in town. They approached the inn, but the demanding crowd was bulging out the door, with each person clamoring for one of the few rooms to be had.

"Joseph realized Mary needed rest – immediately. He couldn't get through the crowd any more than you could get into the gift shop earlier today. You didn't try to find the owner; you just made your way to the first place of respite you could find. And that's what Joseph did too.

"Bad weather looked imminent and threatening. Joseph had to get Mary and the donkey into a place of safety – a place of rest. He had to get her off the saddle and let her recline. He'd go back and fight the crowd soon enough.

"Joseph was a big man, and that was helpful in getting this young girl and her nine-month passenger off the saddle. She was too weary, too ungainly, and too big for her own arms and legs to lift and carry. Joseph led her to a stool to help her escape the weight of her body and the coming new life she carried.

"He led the donkey to the tethering ring and began unfastening the ties for the saddlebags that held their possessions. As he unfastened the last loop to unload the saddlebags, he turned just in time to see Mary's eyes widen with surprise!

"Her water had burst—the baby was coming.

"He quickly made do with some straw and Mary's riding blanket to make a reclining position in the hay. He lifted her with those strong arms of his and carried her ever so gently to the waiting spread. With love in his eyes, Joseph looked deeply into hers and reassured her that all would be well.

"He ran back to the donkey and unloaded their possessions and the water they had been carrying. Then he placed it next to Mary's lips, gave her a sip, and lowered it beside her. He placed her hand on it so it would be within reach and told her he was going for help.

"Joseph ran back to the front of the inn, but the crowd had not subsided. He asked one and then another if they had a room, but no one did. The visitors far outnumbered the rooms. He begged for anyone who had one to share it with a woman giving birth, but surely some thought this a ruse to get a room.

"Joseph didn't dare stay away too long. Unsuccessful in finding a room, he ran full speed back to the stable to Mary's side.

"Yes, the baby came that night and so did the shepherds. But there's more to the story. When the census was completed and the crowds dissipated, there still remained Mary, Joseph, the baby, the innkeeper, and his wife.

"You see, the innkeeper didn't know there was a baby being born in the stable, but he certainly found out. Rumor and gossip fill a small town like Bethlehem, and a baby's cry certainly fills a stable. It would have been impossible to miss."

The Priestly Shepherds

"When the kindly innkeeper heard the news, he wondered to himself, *why would someone give birth in a stable?* If only he had known—and if he could make room – he would have tried to find a proper place for this mother and child.

"He earnestly desired to see if he could help – to find this couple and offer some respite – but where would he begin to search for them? Even though Bethlehem was small, there were a lot of stables to search.

"Nonetheless, if the shepherds found this trio, so could he. When he considered the situation, he realized that these shepherds who shared this amazing story were not like the common herdsmen. No, these were the priestly shepherds!"

"Priestly shepherds?" the pastor queried. "Shepherds who were priests? I've never heard of anything like that before. I thought all the priests worked at the Temple in Jerusalem."

"Oh no!" exclaimed the older man. "These were the priestly shepherds at Migdal Eder."

"Migdal what?" the pastor inquired. "What is – or where is – this Migdal thing?"

The Tower of the Flock may have been used by the priestly shepherds of Bethlehem.

The corners of the innkeeper's mouth began to curve upward, in an ever-so-slight smile. His eyes flashed with new life. His brows raised as he realized this studied pastor had more to learn—much more.

And so he began the lesson for a student of one, and class was now in session.

"To understand Migdal Eder you must understand the story of Rachel and Jacob. Another name for the tower was the memorial to Rachel.

"Go back to the beginning of your Bible—to the book of Genesis and find the man first named Jacob. If you want to read it in your own Bible, you'll find the beginning of this story in Genesis 35.

"Jacob and his wife, Rachel, were traveling from Bethel to Ephrath. And much like Mary in your Christmas story, she too was nine months pregnant. Rachel entered into labor, but with great difficulty, and she would not live to hold the baby she delivered.

"Too weak to look at – much less to hold – her baby, the midwife tried to comfort Rachel with the words, 'You have another son!'

"Rachel felt her life ebbing away and cried out to name the baby 'Ben-oni' which meant, 'son of my sorrow,' and then she died.

"Jacob would not allow this precious baby to live his life with such an unfortunate name and so he renamed this infant 'Ben-jamin,' which meant, 'son of my right hand.'

"Rachel was buried there, on the way to Ephrath. Jacob marked the spot with a memorial to honor his dear wife by setting up a tower. Your Bible calls it the 'pillar of Rachel's tomb,' and it also says that Jacob traveled on from there—from the 'tower of Eder.'

The Pillar of Rachel's Tomb also known as The Tower of Migdal,
The Tower of Eder, or The Tower of the Flock

Jacob built a memorial tower to his wife Rachel, who died after giving birth to their son, Benjamin.
As it crumbled over the centuries it may have been used as a military watchtower. Today, it is unknown
where the tower once stood on the way to Ephrath, somewhere near Bethlehem.

"So, that should answer part of your question. The pillar of Rachel's tomb and the tower of Eder are the same structure—the memorial to Rachel built by Jacob while on his way to Ephrath."

Even though the pastor had often read this story in Genesis 35, it was as though he could see these words for the first time in his life. While he was accustomed to teaching others, he was now being schooled himself. He wondered, *Why haven't I noticed this tower before now? It seemed so irrelevant to me before. What can all of this mean?*

The innkeeper continued. "Throughout the coming years, Rachel's memorial tower eventually gave way to the centuries of weather, wear and tear and even use as a military lookout. The little that remained of the structure later became an important shelter and birthplace for special sheep.

"Even the prophet Micah referred to it as the 'tower of the flock' when he wrote in Micah 4:8…

'And you, O tower of the flock,
hill of the daughter of Zion,
to you shall it come,
the former dominion shall come.'"

The Perfect Lamb

"Wait!" questioned the pastor, "You said these were SPECIAL sheep? What was so special about some sheep at this location?"

"Oh? I thought you'd be familiar with these details," replied the somewhat surprised elder man.

"All of these details are connected—and they all lead to the story of Mary and Joseph. Let me share a few more details and it will all become much clearer."

"Please continue!" said the pastor. "Thank you for sharing this beautiful story."

"You know," the old man smiled at his eager student, "Jerusalem and the Temple are just a short way from here, about eight kilometers, or five miles in your measurement. And you also know that the Temple requires a special annual sacrifice popularly known as the 'Day of Atonement.'

"Every year, the High Priest would select a perfect lamb as an offering to God that would suffice as an act of humility and temporarily atone for our nation's sins against Him. All of Israel recognizes and celebrates this day as one that brings us into a right relationship with God.

"However, that relationship is based on us acknowledging our need for forgiveness and—as God said to Adam and Eve—acknowledging that sin's penalty is death. From our earliest days since the law of Moses, Israel has celebrated this day with the sacrifice of a perfect lamb.

"You see; in approaching a holy God, we must present a 'holy' or special lamb to him. Anything ordinary would not be sufficient, or honoring, to God.

"So, how did the priests find a 'perfect' lamb? Well, they resorted to raising their own. And that is what became of the tower of Eder—it became a place where these special lambs would be bred, born, raised and chosen to be a worthy offering.

"To ensure the lambs met all the requirements of a holy offering, a special group of priests arose whose job it was to watch over, protect and prepare the lambs. The sheepfold had to be within close proximity to Jerusalem so that the High Priest could easily travel there before the great day and return with a suitable lamb."

"This part I know" the pastor interrupted. "The lamb to be sacrificed was to be perfect, without blemish and could have no broken bones."

"Indeed," the innkeeper jumped back in. "Special lambs required special shepherds and those were the priestly shepherds. The rabbinical, priestly shepherds raised the sheep and also inspected the sheep. They did their work very carefully and with great forethought.

"For instance, when the lambs were born, they inspected them meticulously and, as I've said, only those without blemish were selected as possible candidates for the Day of Atonement."

The infant Jesus was wrapped in swaddling clothes and laid in a stone manger used to feed the lambs kept nearby.

Swaddling the Lamb

"After their initial inspection, they also took extreme care that the lambs would not, and could not, become injured. They would wrap them in strips of cloth to protect them from scrambling, falling and becoming injured. After wrapping them, the priests then placed them in a wooden or stone trough. There the lambs would lay still and be cared for. That same stone trough would later serve as a feeding trough for the lambs as they grew. It was called a 'manger.'"

The pastor's eyes lit up with both understanding and excitement! "So, this is what we call SWADDLING the lambs and laying them in a MANGER?"

The well-lit eyes of the pastor were greeted by the delight of the innkeeper. "Absolutely!" replied the innkeeper. "The lambs that were perfect, without blemish, marks, or broken bones were wrapped in swaddling clothes and laid in a manger. I suppose this is sounding familiar to a pastor like yourself?"

The preacher nearly laughed out loud at himself for not having seen this link before. "This sounds so much like the birth of Jesus! Why didn't I know this before?" he exclaimed in amusement and wonder.

"Go on, tell me more," he said to the smiling innkeeper who sat before him.

"As the great Day of Atonement approached, the High Priest would set off to the Tower of Eder, which you now understand was the Pillar of Rachel. There he—along with the priestly shepherds—would carefully choose the one lamb that would qualify to remove the sins of the people.

"Once chosen, the High Priest journeyed back to Jerusalem where he was met by great crowds of people to celebrate that a suitable lamb had been found to atone for their sinful condition. And they looked forward each year to the weight of their sin being lifted from them on this day."

Celebration of the Lamb

"In great anticipation, the crowds would gather to wait for the approach of the Priest as he rode back into the city. They would greet him with shouts of acclamation, shouts of hallelujah and the waving of palm branches in celebration of the spotless lamb.

"Soon, the atoning work provided by the offering of the lamb would come and bring the people release from the bondage to their sins.

"Now, young man," the innkeeper addressed the pastor, "let's add a little more to the story. From where did this lamb come?"

The pastor had a ready answer, "From the Tower of Eder, which was also known as the Tower of the Flock but was originally built by Jacob as a memorial for his wife

Rachel who died in childbirth."

He was starting to see and place all these new pieces of a puzzle into a new picture he had not understood before.

"And where was this tower?" the older man quizzed.

"On the way to Ephrath?" the pastor asked.

"Yes" the aged voice retorted, "but where is Ephrath?"

That brought the entire conversation to a deafening halt. The pastor's happy expression took a sudden turn and transposed into a gasp of bewilderment. Where indeed? the student wondered before speaking. He had not made a habit of studying the geography of Bible lands. He became lost in silent thoughts – with no knowledge to draw upon.

The Tower of the Flock at Migdal Eder

"Allow me to help you in this," came the seasoned voice of one who knew the answer. "I won't give you the answer, but I'll help you find it for yourself."

"Look in the verses of your own Bible. Return to that story of Jacob and Rachel. If you need a little help, go to Genesis 35, verse 19. Why don't you read it aloud so both of us can hear?"

And so, he did. It was still marked from where he had read earlier. "So Rachel died and was buried on the way to Ephrath (that is, Bethlehem)."

"What?!!" gasped the younger man. "Ephrath was Bethlehem?"

"Indeed it was – and is!" the older man chuckled. "Surprised?"

"Am I understanding this right? Rachel died on the way—and just outside of Bethlehem? And Jacob built a memorial to her, which was the Tower of Eder? And the tower eventually housed the lambs to be offered for a sin sacrifice on the Day of Atonement? And the lambs were inspected by priestly shepherds before being wrapped in swaddling clothes and laid in a manger?"

"Ahhhhh, my young friend," replied the teacher. "You are now putting the pieces together in their correct order. You are beginning to see the whole picture!"

"This is making so much sense! It's more than I ever thought—more than I knew and imagined! It's—well—it's just more!"

The Innkeeper moved in a way to indicate he wasn't finished. His story was not yet complete. So he continued in a lower tone, a slower pace and more reverently.

"Yes, Jesus was born in Ephrath—or Bethlehem. And when the original inn-keeper went to find this newborn, where did he go? There would have been so many houses, so many barns and stables to search; but he didn't go to 'any' stable, he went to 'the' stable. And those shepherds to whom the angels appeared: they were no ordinary shepherds; they were priests whose sole function was to provide a spotless lamb to take away the sins—not of a nation—but the sin of the world.

"And remember the naming of Rachel's newborn? She had named him 'son of my sorrow,' but Jacob named him, 'son of my right hand.' So, tell me now, my friend, what does your Bible say in the prophecies about the coming Messiah?"

Foreshadow of the Lamb

The old man leaned in to the young pastor as if he had a special secret. "Doesn't the prophet Isaiah, in the messianic chapter 53, call him a 'man of sorrows?' And didn't Jesus say of himself in Matthew's gospel, chapter 26, that he would be seated at the right hand of his Father? Both of the names that Rachel and Jacob give to this son also foreshadow the coming Messiah, Jesus."

This comment gave the pastor a jolt. "Wait a moment," he said, "you referred to Jesus as the coming Messiah. I thought you're Jewish?!" It was both a statement and a question.

With that, the old Innkeeper wryly smiled and said, "Jesus was the Messiah. He is yours, and mine. Did you think that a man with my connections to the original

Christmas story would not know? All the innkeepers here have known the true identity of the baby born here!"

In an avalanche of information, the preacher who had been seeking for "more" was getting it in abundance. Still, his instructor still had extra to share.

"Let's talk about your typical and traditional view of the original Christmas story. Maybe you need to make a few more adjustments when you retell the story?

"I imagine that when you tell the story, you picture Joseph walking beside Mary as she rides a donkey to Bethlehem. Would that be so?"

"Indeed, it would," replied the preacher.

"Ah, but a donkey was a precious and expensive animal" the teacher went on.

"Here are two things I'd like to point out to you. First, a donkey is not mentioned anywhere in the Biblical story. That idea just arose from someone's artistic license. And, having observed the picture many times, you just assumed the donkey was part of the story.

"Secondly, when Mary and Joseph took Jesus to the Temple for his purification, they were required to present an offering to God. Do you recall what they gave?"

"Yes, I believe it was either a pair of turtledoves or pigeons, wasn't it?"

"You are correct," the seasoned soul replied. "And I hope you recall that this was a poor man's offering. If they had owned a donkey, they could have afforded, and would have given, a more costly gift."

*"And to offer a sacrifice according to that which is said
in the law of the Lord, A pair of turtledoves,
or two young pigeons." ~Luke 2:24*

Just Like a Perfect Lamb

He continued, "So, let's take an inventory of what you have learned so far. Our story takes place in Ephrath, that is a tower in Bethlehem. Jesus was born where the sacrificial lambs were born to become a sacrifice for sin. And just like those lambs, he was wrapped in swaddling clothes. And also like those lambs, he was laid in a manger.

"The shepherds who came to worship him were not common shepherds, they were the priestly shepherds responsible for the flawless lambs to be sacrificed to God in exchange for the forgiveness of sin.

"Again, like those lambs, Jesus was without a broken bone. When soldiers came to break the legs of those on the cross to hasten their death, Jesus was already dead, so they let him be.

"Like the two names given to the boy born to Rachel and Jacob, Jesus was known as both the 'man of sorrow' and one who would 'sit at the right hand of the Father.'

"Now, let me introduce another intriguing point. On the day that the High Priest was to bring the lamb from Bethlehem to Jerusalem, that would have been the day that Jesus rode into Jerusalem and the crowds were already gathered to celebrate the chosen spotless lamb who would die for their sins.

"And, just as they were accustomed to welcoming the High Priest with shouts of acclamation, they welcomed Jesus as he rode into the city. And just as the lamb was slain a few days later, so was Jesus.

"And one more thing. Let's correct something else. Due to a classic Christmas carol, you probably imagine 'cows a lowing' during the birth of Jesus. But, in truth, the Bible doesn't mention anything about other animals being there. That's only another figment of someone's imagination. At the tower of Eder, the only animals around would have been sheep and lambs."

Joseph and the Innkeeper

"Now that you understand the place, the setting and the characters of your Bible story, let me tell you more."

The pastor sat looking at the man intently, his eyes on fire with new revelations about the birth of Jesus. Hardly believing there was more to tell, he asked, "What more could there be?"

"I want to tell you about that which has been handed down through the ages, from father to son, and father to son, for 2,000 years. From generation to generation the innkeeping families have shared this story—the story of our messiah, the story you grew up with—but from another perspective."

"The innkeepers perspective!" cried the pastor. "We never even thought of the innkeeper's perspective. Please continue sharing your profound legacy."

The old man was thrilled at the rapt attention of his student and continued. "When the innkeeper and his wife found the stories to be true, Joseph's family got the first available room. They were in no condition to journey home so soon after giving birth, and so they stayed on at the inn.

"Joseph found his craftsmanship a valuable commodity for trade. He was able to barter his talents for room and board as he helped with a makeover of the inn. The families became family. Both innkeeper and carpenter were more than tradesmen; they had become friends and more."

The Innkeeper Makes Room

"More? How could there be more?" I wondered aloud.

"Aw, read on, but this time from another passage," the old man directed.

This time I turned my Bible to Matthew, chapter 2 and began reading to him in verse 7. "Then Herod, when he had privily called the wise men, enquired of them diligently what time the star appeared. And he sent them to Bethlehem and said, 'Go and search diligently for the young child and when you have found him bring me word again, that I may come and worship him also.'

"When they had heard the king, they departed; and lo, the star, which they saw in the east, went before them, till it came and stood over where the young child was. When they saw the star, they rejoiced with exceeding great joy. And when they had come into the house, they saw the young child with Mary, his mother and fell down and worshipped him—"

"Stop there," the old man said.

I stared into his thickly etched and creased face as if asking for a reason to stop.

"What house?" he questioned. "Whose house do you think that was?" he inquired, with his eyebrows stretching toward his receding hairline. "Go ahead. Tell me whose house was it?"

The text was obvious—Jesus was now a toddler, not the baby which the shepherds had discovered, but this house?

"Nothing much is said about it," I answered. "I suppose I've always assumed that Joseph bought a place in Bethlehem, or back in Nazareth, even though there is no mention of Nazareth at this point in the story."

"It was the innkeeper's house!" The innkeeper was now shouting. "He was no ogre. He wasn't heartless. He wasn't detached. And he wasn't a villain!" The old man shouted with certainty!

"Vilified. Vilified!" he cried out again. "Throughout the ages, this man whose heart and home were opened to Joseph, Mary, and Jesus has been castigated, maligned, and vilified. Not only was their home open to Jesus, but their hearts too!"

And did you take notice that Jesus was now a toddler? Since Herod ordered the killing of all the baby boys under the age of two, we must assume that Mary, Joseph and Jesus may have stayed in Bethlehem for up to two years before moving back to Nazareth.

"How do you know this is true?" I asked squeamishly, as if trying to hold on to a series of assumptions that now looked pitifully frail.

"From what you read; how do you know it's not?" he softly replied.

"Indeed, my friend. Indeed." I pondered.

In following one curious path, in just one afternoon, I had discovered the "more" I'd been longing for. I would soon leave for home with no new trinkets in my luggage but a treasure trove about Christmas in my heart.

Making Room for the Lamb

Maybe the original story of Christmas is more or different than you've ever heard. It seems that many have learned to think of the Innkeeper as a harsh man with no room in his inn for the holy family. Maybe we've just heard the story from only one perspective.

In this story, the Innkeeper opened both his home and his heart to the baby Jesus' family. But what about YOU? Have you made room for Jesus in your life?

Jesus is more than "a good man" or a "moral teacher." He was like a lamb whose death paid a very dear price to get us connected to God. Just as a lamb was sacrificed annually for a temporary forgiveness of sin – Jesus was sacrificed for the sins of the whole world.

Because He came, all peoples from every tongue, tribe and nation are free to make room in their hearts for Him. If you invite Him, He will also forgive your sin, reside within your heart, and reconnect you to God the Father. Not only will he renew you, but He will resurrect your body after you die to be eternally with Him and enjoy Him forever on a restored heaven and earth.

And THAT is what the Christmas story is all about! Jesus left the glory He shared with God the Father in order to restore us to God's family forever. Because He loved us, we can become children of God with Jesus as our brother.

If you sense the need to connect with God as your forever Father, then invite Him in! Do you remember what the heavenly host of angels said to the shepherd's when Jesus was born?

"Glory to God in the highest heaven,
and on earth peace to those on whom his favor rests."

Luke 2:14

The angels were proclaiming God's special love and favor and peace from the burden of sin for anyone who would receive His Son Jesus! God created man for love and fellowship with Him from the very beginning, but sin interrupted the relationship.

Allowing Jesus to forgive your sins and make you new is the first step to reconnect with God. Make room for the Lamb of God that takes away the sin of the world!

The next day he saw Jesus coming toward him, and said,
"Behold, the Lamb of God,
who takes away the sin of the world!"

John 1:29

About the Author

Dr Gerald Robison

Gerald Robison has pastored churches on three continents and trained over 1,200 Bible teachers in over 25 countries. He has served as the international training manager for Walk Thru the Bible ministries, and has founded and cofounded three ministries, including UnveilinGLORY, Cat N Dog Theology, and To All Nations.

He has instructed over 300 classes on World Missions and been a favorite speaker for Perspectives, Steeling the Mind conferences, and missions conferences in the USA and around the world. He has worked with the Issachar Initiative, Finishing the Task, Perspectives, and City for the Nations.

Affectionately known as "Dr. G" to many, he has deep foundations and experience in ministry and missions. Having felt called to Christian ministry while still in high school, he began pursuing an education that took him to Furman and Mercer Universities for a BA in psychology and counseling. He earned a master's degree and Doctor of Ministry at Luther Rice Seminary; he also earned a second master's degree in education and counseling at Georgia State University and continued with graduate studies at the International Institute of Theology and Law sponsored by Simon Greenleaf School of Law and the International Institute of Human Rights sponsored by the University of Strasbourg, France.

Dr. G has a lifelong passion for helping reach people of every tongue, every tribe, and every nation with the message of Christ's love until men and women from every group are gathered in the throne room of God in worship to our heavenly Father and the Lord Jesus Christ.

"After this I looked, and there before me was a great multitude that no one could count, from every nation, tribe, people and language, standing before the throne and before the Lamb. They were wearing white robes and were holding palm branches in their hands.

And they cried out in a loud voice:
"Salvation belongs to our God,
who sits on the throne,
and to the Lamb."

Revelation 7:9-10 (NIV)

Other Works by This Author

A Dog's Tale: An Allegory On What's Gone Wrong in Missions and Evangelism

Because He Liked It: 101 Glimpses of God's Glory in the Animal World

Cat and Dog Prayer: Rethinking Our Conversations With Our Master (with Bob Sjogren)

Cat and Dog Theology Study Guide (with Phil Luckett)

Cat and Dog Theology: Rethinking Our Relationship With Our Master (with Bob Sjogren)

Crocs Eat Rocks: Another 101 Glimpses of God's Glory in the Animal World

Spiritual Warfare: If I'm a Soldier, Where's the War?

The Innkeeper: Another perspective on the original Christmas story

The Story of the Bible (with Bob Sjogren)

Where Did Grandpa Go? That's What I Want To Know

30 Seconds That Can Change Your Life

Before I Was Jesus: 25 secret identities of Jesus the Christ.

30-Seconds That Can Change Your Life

To learn more about Gerald Robison visit www.catndogtheology.com.

Illustrations in order of first appearance

- *Cover Illustration: The Innkeeper in Bethlehem*
- *Ancient Map*
- *Mary and Joseph in Bethlehem*
- *Pastor's Backside*
- *Tour Bus in the Market*
- *Boy in the Market*
- *Alleyway Detour*
- *The Innkeeper at the Window*
- *Donkey*
- *Bethlehem - night sky*
- *Joseph & Mary with donkey*
- *Pastor and Innkeeper at the Table*
- *Joseph & Mary in Bethlehem night*
- *Lambs in the Tower*
- *Tower of Rachel*
- *Lamb in a Meadow*
- *Tower of Migdal*
- *Lambs and Babe in Manger*
- *Hand L with Palm Branch*
- *Hand R with Palm Branch*
- *Pastor in the Chair*
- *Two Turtledoves*
- *Joseph, Mary, Jesus and Innkeeper*
- *Joseph, Mary and Jesus*

About the Illustrator

Jordan Blackstone

Jordan Blackstone is a fine art photographer and artist who loves to paint and a painter who loves photography.

As a creative growing up in Alberta, Canada, Jordan was surrounded by the wild beauty of the prairies and the ruggedness of the Rockies. With these as her backyard and backdrop, they have influenced her style and given her a strong appreciation for the raw beauty of the life around her.

"Don't try to fit me into a particular genre for I am constantly growing and learning," says Blackstone. "While wildlife and nature are my main focal points, I also enjoy working on portraits and graphic design. Each one presents its own unique challenges."

You can find more of Jordan's work at jordan-blackstone.pixels.com.

Author Gerald Robinson has several Exciting Books for Children (and adult who act like children).